UNDERSTANDING THE SPECTRUM

NAVIGATING AUTISM

James D. Chism

Table Of Content

Autism Spectrum Disorder

A complicated neurological disease known as autism spectrum disorder (ASD) is typified by a variety of difficulties with behavior, speech, and social interaction. Since people with ASD can display a wide range of strengths and symptoms, the word "spectrum" is used to characterize the variety in presentation and severity.

The following are the main traits of autism spectrum disorder.

1. Difficulties in Social Communication:
- Difficulty communicating nonverbally, such as through gestures, eye contact, and facial expressions.
- Difficulties in forming and keeping connections.
- Difficulties comprehending social signs and conventions.

2. Repeated Interests and Behaviors:
- Performing acts or movements repeatedly (e.g., rocking, flapping of the hands).
- A strong commitment to customs and traditions.
- A strong concentration on a single interest or subject.

3. Intellectual Sensitivities:
- Increased susceptibility to or avoidance of sensory stimulation (such as sounds, textures, and lights).
- Seeking or refraining from specific sensory encounters.

4. Adaptability and Flexibility:
- Difficulty adjusting to unforeseen or normal changes.
- Difficulties while switching between tasks or settings.

Autism Spectrum Disorder Diagnostic Criteria

Diagnostic guides like the DSM-5 (Diagnostic and Statistical Manual of Mental Disorders, Fifth Edition) and ICD-10 (International Classification of Diseases, Tenth Revision) provide specific criteria that are used to diagnose ASD. Usually, these requirements consist of:

- Long-lasting deficiencies in social interaction and communication in a variety of settings.
- Limited, recurring interests, activities, or behavioral habits.
- Signs that need to be evident from an early age, even though they might not fully materialize until a later developmental stage.

Awareness of the Spectrum

It's critical to understand that autism is a spectrum disorder, with different people having differing degrees of impairment and distinct strengths. Some people with ASD may be exceptionally gifted in certain fields, like music, visual arts, or mathematics, but they may struggle greatly in other facets of daily life.

Development and Autism
Instead of only seeing autism via a deficit-based lens, autism is now more widely understood within the context of neurodiversity, highlighting the importance of neurological differences and encouraging acceptance and accommodation.

Repetitive behaviors, sensory sensitivity, and difficulties with social communication are hallmarks of the complex illness known as autism spectrum disorder. It is essential to acknowledge the variety and uniqueness within the spectrum in order to comprehend and assist those who are autistic.

Variability Of Autism Spectrum Disorder

Individual differences in symptoms, behaviors, strengths, and challenges are hallmarks of autism spectrum disorder (ASD). The term "spectrum" of autism refers to this variety, which reflects the heterogeneous character of the disorder and the various ways it might present in different people.

Scope Variability Contributing Factors
There are multiple factors that contribute to the reported heterogeneity within the autism spectrum:

1. Level of Symptom Severity:
- The severity of ASD symptoms can vary. While some people may just have mild sensory sensitivity issues and social difficulties, others may struggle greatly with behavior, everyday functioning, and communication.

2. Language and Intellectual Capabilities:
There is significant variation in the cognitive profile of people with ASD. Some people may have intellectual difficulties, while others may have ordinary or above-average intelligence (often referred to as high-functioning autism).

3. Concurrent Occurrences:
- Epilepsy, anxiety disorders, attention deficit hyperactivity disorder (ADHD), and gastrointestinal problems are

common co-occurring symptoms in people with ASD. The intensity and existence of these disorders may also have an impact on the autistic phenotype.

4. Intellectual Sensitivities:
- Spectrum diversity is also influenced by sensory sensitivity. While some people may actively seek out sensory stimulation, others may be hypersensitive to specific sensory stimuli (such as loud noises or textures).

5. Skills in Communication:
The communication skills of people with ASD differ greatly from one another. Some people can communicate verbally and nonverbally, whereas others may only speak in limited sentences.

6. Interests and Behavioral Patterns:
- Individuals with ASD may differ greatly in the frequency and severity of repeated behaviors, specific interests, and regular observance.

Awareness of the Continuum
The idea of the autism spectrum highlights the fact that autism is a continuum of qualities rather than a single, set condition. On one end of the range, people could have less severe symptoms and perform quite well in mainstream environments, while on the other, people might need a lot of help just to get by on a daily basis.

Repercussions for Identification and Management
Because the autism spectrum is so diverse, individualized diagnosis and intervention strategies are crucial. It emphasizes the requirement for customized evaluations

that take into account the special requirements, difficulties,
and abilities of every individual with ASD.

Gratitude for Neurodiversity
Promoting neurodiversity—a theory that acknowledges
and values individual differences in neurology—requires
embracing spectrum variability. A neurodiversity
viewpoint highlights the value of varied cognitive profiles
and talents among persons with ASD, as opposed to
concentrating only on deficiencies.

One of the main characteristics of autism spectrum
disorder is spectrum variability. Understanding the
complexity of ASD and offering appropriate support and
interventions catered to the specific needs of each person
on the spectrum require an appreciation of this
heterogeneity, which must be acknowledged.

Chapter 2: Reasons And Danger Elements

Genetic Factors

Numerous genetic variables are known to play a significant role in the development of autism spectrum disorder (ASD), with a substantial hereditary component. Although research has revealed a number of genetic pathways and risk factors connected with ASD, the precise genetic underpinnings of the disorder remain complex and poorly understood.

Important Genetic Influence Points:

1. Bioavailability:
- Research on twins and families has repeatedly demonstrated the high heritability rate of ASD, suggesting a major role for genetic variables in its development. Compared to fraternal twins, the chance that the other twin will be affected if one identical twin has ASD is significantly higher.

2. Genetic Alterations and Variants:
- ASD has been linked to a wide range of genetic mutations and variations. These can include both frequent genetic alterations (like copy number variations, or CNVs) and uncommon genetic variants (like single nucleotide polymorphisms, or SNPs).

3. The Function of Particular Genes:
- A number of genes have been found to be strongly associated with ASD. Genes related to synapse function,

neural growth, and neuron-to-neurons transmission, for instance, are frequently implicated.

4. De Novo vs. Inherited Mutations:
- Genetic mutations inherited from parents may increase the chance of ASD. Furthermore, de novo mutations—mutations that occur naturally in the sperm or egg, or during early development—have an impact, especially when no family history of ASD exists.

5. Intricate Genetic Structure:
- It is thought that the genetic architecture of ASD is complicated, including the interaction of several genes and genetic pathways. The great variation in symptoms and presentations seen in people with ASD is partly due to this complexity.

Interactions with the Environment:
Even though genetics predominates in ASD, it's crucial to remember that genetic variables interact with environmental circumstances. In genetically vulnerable people, environmental factors like early life experiences, mother health during pregnancy, and prenatal exposures can also play a role in the development and manifestation of ASD.

Repercussions for Research and Diagnosis:
Research into prospective treatments, genetic counseling, and diagnosis are all significantly impacted by our growing understanding of the genetic foundations of ASD. In clinical settings, the use of genetic testing—including whole genome sequencing and chromosomal microarray analysis—is growing in order to pinpoint certain genetic variations linked to ASD.
Autism spectrum disorder development is greatly

influenced by genetics. Even though ASD has a complicated and diverse genetic landscape, research is still being done to identify the genetic pathways that underlie the disorder. The ultimate goal of this study is to improve ASD diagnosis, treatment, and support for affected individuals and their families.

Environmental Factors

Environmental variables influence the expression and risk of autism spectrum disorder (ASD), even if heredity plays a major part in the condition's development. Many non-genetic factors can have an impact on neurodevelopment throughout critical stages of prenatal and early postnatal life, and these factors are referred to as environmental impacts.

Important environmental variables linked to ASD include:

1. Living Conditions:
- Maternal Health: Pregnancy-related maternal health can affect a child's risk of ASD. Increased risk of ASD has been associated with factors including immune system dysregulation, usage of certain drugs (like valproate), exposure to environmental pollutants (like pesticides and air pollution), and maternal illnesses (like influenza and rubella).
Prenatal Nutrition: A healthy mother's consumption of vital vitamins and nutrients (such as folic acid) is crucial for the development of the fetus's brain and may reduce the incidence of ASD.

2. Difficulties with Birth:
A higher risk of ASD has been linked to labor and delivery

complications such oxygen deprivation or low birth weight.

3. First-Life Exposures:
Exposure to Environmental Toxins: Research has examined the possible link between the development of ASD and environmental factors experienced during early life, including air pollutants, heavy metals (such as lead and mercury), and endocrine-disrupting chemicals.
Parental Age and Birth Spacing: It has been determined that shorter birth intervals between siblings and advanced parental age at conception may be environmental risk factors for ASD.

4. Behavioral and Social Factors:
Parental Support and Interaction: Early parent-child interactions and supportive family contexts have a significant impact on the social and cognitive development of children diagnosed with autism spectrum disorders.
- Access to Services and Interventions: The availability of community support, educational materials, and early intervention services can have a major impact on the results for people with ASD.

Interactions Between Gene and Environment:

It is crucial to understand that the risk and variability of ASD are typically influenced by complicated interactions between hereditary and environmental factors. ASD is linked to altered neurodevelopmental trajectories that result from specific environmental exposures being more susceptible to certain genetic vulnerabilities.

Implications and Research Challenges:

Because environmental exposures are complex and variable, studying environmental factors in relation to ASD poses special problems. To gain a deeper understanding of the combined effects of environmental factors on the development and risk of ASD, longitudinal studies and large-scale population-based research initiatives are required.

The multifactorial etiology of autism spectrum disorder (ASD) is influenced by environmental factors that combine with genetic predispositions to affect neurodevelopmental outcomes. Improving our knowledge of these environmental factors is crucial for developing early interventions, support services, and preventive measures that maximize outcomes for people with ASD.

The Screening and Early Symptoms

Observing behavioral, communicative, and developmental trends in newborns and toddlers that can point to abnormal neurodevelopment is important in identifying the early indications of autism spectrum disorder (ASD). Even though each child develops at their own rate, the following warning signs call for further attention and ASD testing:

1. Difficulties with Social Communication:
- Insufficient or nonexistent eye contact during conversations
- Failure to react to names or trouble interpreting social cues
- Little desire to socialize or play games like peek-a-boo with others

2. Difficulties in Communication:
- Limited or delayed speech development (for example, no words by 16 months, or no babble by 12 months).
- Having trouble starting or continuing conversations
- Odd linguistic patterns, such as echolalia or repeated words

3. Recurring Patterns and Limited Pursuits:
- Making repetitive motions, such as rocking or flapping one's hands.
- A strong concentration on one or more interesting objects or subjects
- Resistance to alterations in customs or practices

4. Intellectual Sensitivities:
- Atypical responses to sensory inputs, such as hypersensitivity to particular lights, noises, or textures
- Seeking or avoiding tactile stimulation (such as hands fluttering close to eyes or items whirling).

Diagnostic and Screening Instruments

In order to find any indications of autism, early screening for ASD includes a methodical evaluation of developmental milestones and behaviors. In pediatric healthcare settings, a number of standardized screening instruments are frequently employed to assess social communication abilities and identify potential early signs of ASD:

1. The M-CHAT, or Modified Checklist for Autism in Toddlers:
- A popular screening instrument that parents or other caregivers use to evaluate their toddlers' behavior and social communication between the ages of 16 and 30 months. Positive M-CHAT results frequently call for a healthcare provider to do additional assessment.

2. Symbolic Behavior Scales (CSBS) and Communication:
- A thorough developmental examination that rates newborns' and toddlers' social and communication abilities.

3. Screening Instrument for Autism in Young Children and Toddlers (STAT):
- A method of direct observation used by qualified experts to evaluate young children's play, mimicry, and social communication abilities.

The Significance of Prompt Intervention

Timely intervention and support services are made possible by the early identification of ASD through screening. Children with ASD can benefit from early intervention programs that support communication, social interaction, and adaptive abilities. These programs include speech therapy, occupational therapy, and behavioral interventions like Applied Behavior Analysis.

Teamwork Is Key
A team effort including parents, caregivers, physicians, educators, and developmental experts is needed to screen for ASD. Early detection and treatments for autism spectrum disorder need careful observation of developmental milestones and timely referral for additional assessment if concerns are raised.
Implementing screening techniques and recognizing ASD symptoms early are essential for identifying children who might benefit from early intervention programs. Optimal outcomes for individuals with autism spectrum disorder can be supported by healthcare professionals and caregivers through timely screenings and raising awareness of early indications.

Diagnostic Process
1. First Assessment and Recommendation:
A referral from a pediatrician, psychologist, educator, or parent/caregiver who has noticed possible indications of ASD in the person is frequently the first step in the diagnostic process. Atypical behaviors, delayed developmental milestones, and communication issues can all be cause for concern.

2. In-depth Developmental Evaluation:
- A thorough evaluation is carried out by a multidisciplinary team that may include physicians, child psychologists, occupational therapists, speech-language pathologists, and developmental specialists. This evaluation entails:
- Examining the family medical history, developmental history, milestones, and prenatal and perinatal variables.
- Monitoring the person's activities, social relationships, and communication abilities in various contexts (e.g., home, school).
- Using standardized assessment instruments and questionnaires to collect data on adaptive functioning, repetitive habits, social communication, and sensory sensitivity.

3. DSM-5 or ICD-10 Diagnostic Criteria:
- The DSM-5 or ICD-10 provide specific diagnostic criteria that serve as a guide for the evaluation. In addition to limited, repetitive patterns of behavior, interests, or hobbies, an individual must demonstrate ongoing difficulties in social communication and interaction in order to be diagnosed with autism spectrum disorder (ASD). Early childhood symptoms that significantly affect day-to-day functioning are required.

4. Group Assessment and Prognosis:
- The diagnostic team reviews the assessment results collectively. Based on the existence and intensity of ASD symptoms as well as the individual's particular strengths and difficulties, a consensus is achieved.

5. Health and Genetic Assessment:
- To rule out other underlying medical problems or genetic syndromes that can present with symptoms similar to ASD,

further medical and genetic evaluations may be advised in specific cases.

6. Comments and Suggestions:
- The person and their family receive comments after the diagnostic evaluation. Together with recommendations for interventions, therapies, and support services catered to the specific requirements of the individual, an official diagnosis of ASD is conveyed.

7. Creating a Customized Treatment Program:
A tailored treatment plan is created to address certain ASD-related areas of difficulty based on the results of the diagnostic exam. Early intervention programs, speech, occupational, and behavioral therapies, as well as educational accommodations, may fall under this category.

Value of Early Identification and Intervention:
It is essential to diagnose ASD early in order to start interventions on time, which can improve quality of life and promote the best possible outcomes. Early intervention programs work best when they are used in early life, during a crucial stage of neurodevelopment.
In order to establish if a person meets the diagnostic criteria for autism spectrum disorder, a thorough assessment of the person's behavior, communication, and developmental history is conducted as part of the diagnostic process. For people with ASD to receive the right interventions and an accurate diagnosis, caregivers and medical experts must work together.

Chapter 4: Autism Spectrum Disorder Types

The Asperger's Syndrome

The 1940s saw the emergence of Asperger's syndrome, named for Austrian doctor Hans Asperger, a unique form of autism marked by comparatively milder symptoms and maintained language development. It was believed to be a subtype of autism, with affected people displaying certain behavioral characteristics and difficulties interacting with others.

Important characteristics of Asperger's syndrome:

1. Difficulties in Social Interaction:
- People with Asperger's syndrome frequently have trouble interacting with others in social situations. They may also have trouble keeping eye contact, deciphering nonverbal clues, and reading body language and facial expressions.
- They could find it difficult to make and maintain relationships, preferring to engage in solitary pursuits or interactions focused on certain interests.

2. Discrepancies in Communication:
Despite having full vocabulary and language development, people with Asperger's syndrome can have difficulty using pragmatic language (e.g., recognizing sarcasm, taking turns in conversation, using proper tone and pitch).
- They might speak in a formal or verbose manner, frequently concentrating on a few interesting subjects in great detail.

3. Repetitive Behaviors and Limited Interests:
Asperger's syndrome sufferers, like other people on the
autism spectrum, frequently exhibit strong interests in
particular subjects (such as trains, dinosaurs, or
mathematics) and participate in repetitive actions or
routines (such as lining up things or following rigid
timetables).

4. Intellectual Sensitivities:
- People with Asperger's syndrome frequently have sensory
sensitivity, which is an increased sensitivity or aversion to
particular sensory stimuli like bright lights, loud noises, or
particular textures.

Prognosis and Modifications to the Classification:

Before the 2013 revision of the DSM-5, Asperger's
syndrome was considered a different diagnosis from
autism. It was distinguished by a profile of social
difficulties, repetitive activities, and limited interests in
addition to the lack of notable language deficits. Asperger's
syndrome and other associated pervasive developmental
disorders, however, were merged into the more inclusive
category of autism spectrum disorder (ASD) with the
release of the DSM-5 update.
Ongoing Comprehension and Assistance:

Even if the word "Asperger's syndrome" is no longer used
in a diagnostic sense, many people nevertheless identify
with the particular traits linked to Asperger's and may
prefer to refer to their experiences using this name.
Comprehending these distinctive characteristics can assist
in customizing interventions and support services to fulfill
the requirements of people with comparable profiles on the
autism spectrum.

Within the autistic spectrum, Asperger's syndrome is a unique profile that is defined by particular difficulties with behavior, social communication, and narrow interests. Even though the diagnostic categories have changed, an awareness of the distinctive characteristics linked to Asperger's can help develop supportive strategies that encourage empathy, acceptance, and self-determination for those who share these characteristics.

Pervasive Developmental Disorder (PDD)

A collection of illnesses known as pervasive developmental disorder (PDD) are distinguished by deficits in behavior, social interaction, and communication. While the diseases included in the PDDs group had some commonalities, there were significant variances in the disorders' severity and particular symptoms. PDDs were used to categorize a number of disorders, including:

1. Specific Disorders of Autism (ASD):
- ASD is a broad category of neurodevelopmental disorders marked by difficulties with social interaction, repetitive habits, and narrow interests. The broad range of symptoms and severity seen in people with ASD is reflected in the term "autism spectrum."

2. Depressive Illness:
Asperger's syndrome was identified by distinct difficulties in social interaction and communication, together with milder symptoms than classic autism. - Language development was intact in Asperger's syndrome. As previously mentioned, the DSM-5 now classifies Asperger's syndrome under the more general heading of ASD.

3. Disintegrative Childhood Disorder (CDD):
- CDD is an uncommon disorder that usually develops
after a period of normal development and is marked by
severe regression in a number of developmental domains,
such as language, motor skills, and social skills.

4. PDD-NOS, or PDD-Not Otherwise Specified:
When a person met some but not all of the precise criteria
for autism or other pervasive developmental disorders,
PDD-NOS was used as the diagnosis. It was a residual
category for those with symptoms that were either atypical
or below threshold.

Diagnostic Classification Evolution:
Significant changes were made to the diagnostic standards
and categorization of autism and related disorders with the
release of the DSM-5 in 2013. Individual diseases like
autism spectrum disorder (ASD) were reclassified and
diagnosed based on particular criteria relating to social
communication, repetitive behaviors, and symptom
intensity. The term "pervasive developmental disorder"
was deleted as a diagnostic category.

Present Diagnosis Method:
At the moment, the DSM-5's list of symptoms—which
includes their presence and severity—is used by doctors to
diagnose autism spectrum disorder (ASD). These include
confined, recurring patterns of behavior, interests, or
hobbies, as well as deficiencies in social communication
and engagement. The broad range of symptoms and
manifestations that are included in the diagnosis of ASD
highlights the variety of experiences that people with the
disorder have.
Although it is no longer a diagnostic category, "pervasive
developmental disorder" once referred to a collection of

problems marked by difficulties with behavior, socialization, and communication. A more sophisticated knowledge of these problems has resulted from the evolution of diagnostic classification, with a focus on tailored assessment and diagnosis based on particular criteria connected to neurodevelopmental conditions associated with autism spectrum disorder (ASD).

Childhood Disintegrative Disorder

A period of typical growth is followed by a sharp and abrupt regression in developmental skills, which is the hallmark of the rare disorder known as Childhood Disintegrative Disorder (CDD). The start of symptoms usually happens after two years of age, usually between the ages of three and four, however it can happen later. In the DSM-5, CDD is now included in the more inclusive neurodevelopmental disorders category, rather of being listed as a separate pervasive developmental disorder.

Clinical Disintegrative Disorder Key Features:

1. Reduction in Skill:
- A severe and quick loss of previously learned developmental skills in a variety of domains, such as play skills, social interaction, language (both expressive and receptive), fine and gross motor skills, and adaptive behaviors (like dressing and using the restroom), is the defining characteristic of CDD.

2. Time of Regression:
- Typically, parents and caregivers describe a phase of normal growth during which the child meets developmental milestones including talking, babbling, socializing, and playing correctly. The next stage is

regression, which is marked by a deterioration in these abilities.

3. Diagnosis:
- Children diagnosed with CDD may display symptoms that are comparable to those of autism spectrum disorder (ASD), such as sensory sensitivity, communication deficits, repetitive behaviors (e.g., stereotypic movements), difficulties in social interaction (e.g., lack of eye contact, limited social engagement), and language loss.

4. Medical Requirements:
A diagnosis of CDD necessitates the fulfillment of particular requirements listed in diagnostic guides like the DSM-5. These requirements include a marked decline in several developmental domains and a start before a predetermined age (e.g., before age 10).

Diagnosis Differential:
It's critical to distinguish Childhood Disintegrative Disorder (CDD) from other diseases including Rett syndrome, autism spectrum disorder (ASD), and other genetic or neurological conditions that might manifest as regression. To establish the diagnosis of CDD and rule out underlying medical causes, thorough medical and developmental testing are required.

Oversight and Assistance:
Multidisciplinary methods, such as speech therapy, occupational therapy, behavioral therapies, and educational assistance, are used in the management of childhood disintegrative disorder. In order to address residual abilities and support adaptive functioning in afflicted individuals, early intervention is essential.

Surveillance:
A cautious prognosis is linked to childhood disintegrative disorder because the loss of abilities is often severe and can cause substantial lifetime deficits. Individual characteristics including the degree of regression, residual skills, and response to therapies all affect long-term results.

After a period of regular development, children with Childhood Disintegrative condition (CDD), a rare neurodevelopmental condition, exhibit severe regression in several developmental domains. While there are many parallels between CDD and autism spectrum disease (ASD), CDD is different from ASD in that it develops suddenly and rapidly loses skills. Supporting people with CDD and their families requires early detection, precise diagnosis, and all-encompassing interventions.

Chapter 5: Awareness Of the Spectrum

Behavior and Ability

Autism Spectrum Disorder (ASD) is typified by a wide range of behaviors, skills, and difficulties that differ greatly among cases. Numerous factors, including genetic predispositions, neurodevelopmental trajectories, environmental effects, and individual strengths and weaknesses, contribute to this heterogeneity. To comprehend the spectrum of behavior and skills associated with ASD, one must acknowledge the following elements:

1. Social Interaction and Communication:

- High-Functioning ASD: Some people with ASD, who are sometimes referred to as "high-functioning," may possess comparatively strong cognitive and verbal skills. Even if they can have trouble interpreting nonverbal clues and social cues, they may be able to have discussions, use complicated vocabulary, and show a desire for social connection.
Nonverbal or Minimal Speech: On the other extreme of the spectrum, people with ASD may have minimal or no speech (nonverbal ASD) and face considerable difficulties when interacting with others. They might rely on augmentative and alternative communication (AAC) devices, picture cards, gestures, or other non-verbal means of communicating.

2. Interests and Repetitive Behaviors:

Narrow or Intense Interests: A lot of people with ASD have intense hobbies or interests in particular subjects, frequently exhibiting in-depth knowledge and intensity in these areas. These passions can serve as a source of support and inspiration for education and involvement.

- Repetitive Movements: Some people use repetitive motions or actions (such rocking or flapping the hands) as a coping mechanism or a means of self-regulation. The frequency and severity of these actions can vary.

3. Sensitivity to Sensations:

- Sensory Seeking or Avoidance: Individuals with ASD may be sensitive to certain stimuli, such as loud noises, bright lights, or particular textures, and may either seek out or avoid certain sensory experiences, such as spinning objects or visual patterns.

4. Learning and Cognition Profiles:

- Intellectual Abilities: ASD has been linked to a broad spectrum of intellectual abilities, including average or above-average intelligence (high IQ) and intellectual impairment (ID). Some people might be particularly good at arithmetic, music, or the visual arts.

5. Adaptive Operation:

Everyday Living Skills: The capacity to carry out everyday tasks on one's own, including getting dressed, taking care of oneself, and preparing meals, is referred to as adaptive functioning. The degree of independence in adaptive abilities might differ greatly amongst people with autism spectrum disorder.

6. Behavioral Difficulties:

- Emotional Regulation: People with ASD frequently struggle with impulse control, emotional regulation, and stress or anxiety management. To address these issues, behavioral interventions and support are frequently used.

7. Personal Advantages and Adaptability:

- Unique Abilities: The distinctiveness and resilience of every person with ASD are influenced by their distinct abilities, talents, and personality traits. It is crucial to acknowledge and support these strengths in order to encourage personal development and wellbeing.

The term autism spectrum disorder (ASD) refers to a wide variety of behaviors, skills, and difficulties that are indicative of the individual experiences and traits of those who have the condition. We can embrace inclusive and person-centered approaches that support the various needs and potential of individuals with ASD across the spectrum by acknowledging and valuing this variety.

Advantages Strengths and difficulties

1. Expertise and Specialized Interests:
- ASD sufferers may have strong interests in particular subjects or fields of study. They frequently display extraordinary concentration, meticulousness, and in-depth knowledge of their subjects. Specialized knowledge can result in exceptional skills and knowledge in certain domains.

2. Skills for Visual Thinking and Problem-Solving:
- Some people with ASD are quite good at spatial reasoning and visual thinking. They could exhibit original methods for approaching assignments with visual or spatial components, as well as creative problem-solving abilities.

3. Recall and Focus on Detail:
- Individuals with ASD may have excellent recall abilities, especially when it comes to factual knowledge or specifics pertaining to their interests. They frequently pick up on minute details that others might miss, which is useful in some occupations or pursuits.

4. Reliability and Open Communication:
- People with ASD are frequently recognized for their openness and directness in communicating. They may interact with a strong sense of integrity and have a tendency to express what they mean.

5. Devotion and Perseverance:
- Many people with ASD show incredible perseverance and commitment while pursuing interests or ambitions. They might demonstrate a strong will to overcome obstacles and reach goals.

6. Special Creative Skills:
- Some people with ASD have special creative skills, such as artistic aptitude, musical aptitude, or creative problem-solving across a range of fields. These artistic abilities can be developed and honored.

The following are challenges related to autism spectrum disorder (ASD):

1. Communication and Social Challenges:
- Social relationships and peer interactions might be hampered by difficulties comprehending nonverbal cues, social cues, and reciprocal exchanges. Communication may also be impacted by expressive and receptive language difficulties.

2. Overload and Sensory Sensitivities:
- Sensory sensitivity, including hypersensitivity to light, sounds, textures, tastes, and scents, is common in people with ASD. In circumstances that are overpowering, sensory overload can cause discomfort, anxiety, or meltdowns.

3. Repeated Actions and Patterns:
- Repetitive behaviors (such as hand flapping and rocking) and strict routines or rituals can make it difficult to be flexible and adjust to change, which can have an impact on day-to-day activities and social interactions.

4. Difficulties in Executive Functioning:
- Academic achievement, work completion, and adaptive abilities can all be negatively impacted by difficulties with executive functions, which include planning, organization, flexibility, and impulse control.

5. Controlling Emotions and Stress:
- People with ASD may have difficulty controlling their emotions and handling stress, which can result in elevated levels of anxiety, annoyance, or emotional dysregulation.

6. How to Get Help and Services:
For people with ASD and their families, having limited access to specialized programs, therapies, and accommodations that are suited to their specific requirements can present extra difficulties.

People with autism spectrum disorder (ASD) have special strengths and encounter certain difficulties that affect their day-to-day activities and relationships. Through an emphasis on strengths, development of talents, and tailored treatments and support for problems, we can enable people with ASD to live happy, purposeful lives and make valuable contributions to society with their special insights and skills.

Chapter 6: Treating Autism Spectrum Disorder

Therapeutic Approaches for the Management of Autism Spectrum Disorder (ASD)

1. ABA, or Applied Behavior Analysis:
- ABA is a methodical, empirically supported therapy aimed at enhancing particular behaviors and abilities. In order to encourage independence, it entails segmenting desirable behaviors into smaller tasks, rewarding successful attempts, and gradually reducing supports. ABA focuses on a number of areas, including social skills, communication, adaptive behavior, and the decrease of problematic behaviors.

2. Language and Speech Therapy:
- The goal of speech-language therapy is to enhance social communication, pragmatic language usage (using language in social situations), speech production, and language comprehension. Speech-language pathologists employ a range of strategies, including social skills instruction, visual aids, and augmentative and alternative communication (AAC) systems.

3. OT (Occupational Therapy):
- Occupational therapists assist people with ASD in enhancing their engagement in everyday activities, motor coordination, self-care abilities, and sensory processing. To improve independence and functional abilities, occupational therapy (OT) methods may involve fine motor exercises, self-regulation techniques, sensory integration therapy, and adaptive equipment.

4. Teaching Social Skills:
- The goal of social skills training is to impart basic interpersonal behaviors and social skills to people with ASD, like taking turns, striking up conversations, reading social cues, and managing emotions. Group-based therapy offers controlled environments in which to practice social interactions.

5. CBT: Cognitive-behavioral therapy
- CBT is a treatment technique that assists people with ASD in addressing repeated behaviors, managing anxiety, and creating coping mechanisms for emotional control. Cognitive restructuring, relaxation methods, and behavior modification tactics are examples of CBT procedures.

6. Medications for Development:
- For young children with ASD, developmental treatments place a strong emphasis on early intervention and comprehensive care. Through play-based and family-centered approaches, these therapies aim to promote overall development, including cognitive, verbal, social, and motor skills.

7. Interventions Mediated by Parents:
Programs for parent coaching and training enable parents and other caregivers to use successful tactics and interventions both at home and in public places. These programs build advocacy and support for their child's needs, as well as positive behavior management strategies and improved parent-child interactions.

8. Personalized Education Plans (IEPs) and Educational Supports:
Creating individualized education plans (IEPs) that are specific to the strengths and learning requirements of kids

with ASD is the first step in educational interventions. To maximize academic and social success, educational aids may include treatments incorporated into school settings, customized instruction, and accommodations.

9. Visual and Structural Supports:
- Understanding, organization, and predictability can be improved for people with ASD through the use of structured and visual aids, such as visual schedules, social stories, and picture-based communication systems (like PECS), which can help with behavior control and communication.

The goal of therapeutic interventions for autism spectrum disorder (ASD) is to improve the quality of life for people of all ages by fostering skill development and supporting individual growth. When these interventions are customized to each person's needs, applied regularly, and incorporated into everyday activities and surroundings, they work best. To optimize therapy therapies' effects and foster positive outcomes for individuals with ASD, cooperation between professionals, families, and caregivers is crucial.

Educational Strategies

1. Organized Instruction and Visual Aids:
- To improve comprehension and predictability, structured education methods, including the TEACCH (Treatment and Education of Autistic and Related Communication-Hampered Children) approach, place an emphasis on visual supports, planned schedules, and task organization. People with ASD can manage routines, transitions, and activities more independently with the use

of visual supports, such as visual schedules, visual signals, and visual task instructions.

2. ABA (Applied Behavior Analysis) in the classroom:
- ABA principles are used in educational settings to target social relationships, behavioral problems, communication skills, and specific learning objectives. Systematic approaches, reinforcement tactics, and data-driven approaches are used in ABA-based educational programs to support the development of skills and behavior control.

3. Personalized Learning Programs (PLEPs):
- Individualized Education Plans (IEPs) are customized lesson plans created to meet the specific requirements, objectives, and accommodations of students with ASD. In inclusive or specialized educational environments, IEPs provide precise learning goals, tailored services, and support to help students advance academically and socially.

4. Interventions Mediated by Peers:
Peer-mediated therapies pair kids with ASD with peers who are usually developing in order to promote social interactions and inclusion. These interventions use organized activities, cooperative learning, and constructive peer interactions to improve peer relationships, social skills, and mutual understanding.

5. Teaching Social Skills and Peer Training:
- Social skills instruction concentrates on imparting to individuals with ASD particular social abilities and behaviors, such as striking up discussions, forming friendships, recognizing social cues, and settling disputes. Peer education programs involve teaching classmates about autism and cultivating supportive relationships,

empathy, and acceptance throughout the school community.

6. Sensor-Friendly Settings and Supports for Sensations:
- Creating sensory-friendly surroundings that accommodate sensitivity and lessen sensory overload is emphasized in educational approaches for ASD. Sensory aids encourage comfort, self-regulation, and engagement in school activities. Examples of these include sensory breaks, quiet areas, and sensory gadgets like fidget toys.

7. Inclusive and Collaborative Methods:
- Multidisciplinary teams made up of teachers, therapists, specialists, and families collaborate to create inclusive learning environments that cater to the many needs of students with ASD through collaborative educational techniques. Coordinated therapies, pooled knowledge, and all-encompassing assistance between academic and therapeutic domains are made possible by collaboration.

8. Learning Supported by Technology:
- Interactive apps, digital platforms, and assistive devices are examples of educational technology that can help students with ASD learn and communicate. Personalized instruction, visual aids, and interactive resources are provided by technology-assisted learning tools to improve engagement and skill development.

The various evidence-based practices, strategies, and interventions used in educational approaches for autism spectrum disorder (ASD) are designed to meet the individual learning needs and strengths of individuals with ASD. Academic achievement, social interaction, and overall success for students with ASD within educational settings are the goals of educational approaches, which are implemented through the use of individualized education plans, the creation of inclusive environments, and the collaboration of educators and stakeholders.

Family Dynamics

1. Effect on Family Connections:
- The diagnosis of autism spectrum disorder (ASD) can have an effect on family dynamics and relationships as parents, siblings, and extended family members deal with difficulties in comprehending and helping the person with ASD. The demands of caregiving can cause siblings to feel a range of emotions, from empathy and understanding to feelings of neglect or frustration.

2. Stress and Coping in Parents:
- Raising a child with autism spectrum disorder (ASD) can be emotionally and physically taxing, which increases stress and caregiving obligations. While juggling the needs of their child with ASD with other family responsibilities, parents may feel uncertain, guilty, and alone.

3. Difficulties in Communication:
- ASD-related communication issues, such as restricted verbal expression, trouble reading social cues, and repetitive speech patterns, can affect how families communicate. To promote understanding and interaction, family members might need to modify the way they communicate and employ new tactics.

4. Modifications to Family Activities and Routines:
- Due to the individual's distinct needs and preferences, family routines, schedules, and activities may need to be modified when an ASD is present. Daily routine adjustments can have an impact on family dynamics and

call for everyone in the family to be adaptable and flexible.

5. Positive and Financial Aspects:
- Accessing specialized services, therapies, and educational support for individuals with ASD may present financial challenges for families. Practical factors that affect employment, household management, and overall family stability include time commitments and caregiving responsibilities.

6. Sibling Bonds and Assistance:
- The development and relationships of siblings of people with ASD may be impacted in both positive and negative ways. Through their experiences, siblings may grow in empathy, tolerance, and resilience, but they may also need more emotional support and care from parents.

7. Support Systems and Coping Mechanisms:
- Resilience and wellbeing within ASD-affected families are promoted by effective coping strategies and support systems. Families can overcome obstacles and develop resilience by having access to peer support groups, professional counseling, respite care services, and community resources.

8. Approaches Based on Strengths and Family Involvement:
- Building supportive environments for people with ASD and promoting positive family dynamics require an understanding of and ability to utilize the strengths, resources, and resilience of the family. Participation of families in treatment planning, interventions, and advocacy improves results and gives them more authority as co-travelers on the path of ASD.
Autism spectrum disorder (ASD) patients' particular needs,

difficulties, and strengths influence the dynamics within their families. Professionals and support networks can provide specialized interventions, resources, and strategies to support positive family dynamics, resilience, and well-being by having a thorough understanding of the effects of ASD on family relationships, communication patterns, and daily routines.

Community Resources

1. Organizations that Support Autism:
Regional and national autism support groups offer advocacy, resources, and information to people with ASD and their families. These organizations facilitate family connections, experience sharing, and access to community-based services by providing workshops, support groups, helplines, and online forums.

2. Schools and Educational Services:
- Students with ASD have specific learning needs that are met by inclusive classrooms, special education programs, and community-based schools. Individualized education plans (IEPs), speech, occupational, and behavioral therapies, as well as social skills instruction, can all be included in educational services.

3. Medical Services:
- Community-based therapeutic services are essential in helping people with ASD develop their communication skills, motor coordination, sensory integration, and behavior control. These services include speech-language therapy, occupational therapy, physical therapy, and behavioral therapy (such as applied behavior analysis, or ABA).

4. Medical Professionals and Experts:
Having access to medical professionals with expertise in developmental pediatrics, neurology, psychiatry, and psychology is crucial for the thorough assessment, diagnosis, and continuing care of people with ASD. These experts provide advice on medical interventions, medication management, and diagnostic evaluations.

5. Social and Recreational Activities:
Participating in community-based recreational programs, sports leagues, art classes, music therapy, and social clubs offers people with ASD the chance to make friends in inclusive environments, learn social skills, and participate in structured activities.

6. Education and Assistance for Parents:
- Parent training programs and support groups provide parents and other caregivers of people with ASD with information, direction, and emotional support. These resources offer methods for handling difficulties, navigating care systems, speaking up for their child's needs, and establishing relationships with other families.

7. Services for Employment and Transition:
Community-based services that concentrate on supported employment, job placement, vocational training, and transition planning assist people with ASD in adjusting to adulthood and navigating opportunities for independent living, post-secondary education, and employment.

8. Services for Family Support and Respite Care:
- Respite care programs provide families with individuals with ASD with short-term relief and support, enabling caregivers to take breaks and tend to their own needs. Family support services help people make connections

with community-based supports, navigate care systems, and obtain financial resources.

9. Legal and Advocacy Resources:
- Autism advocacy groups and legal services help families understand their legal rights under disability laws (such as the Americans with Disabilities Act (ADA) and the Individuals with Disabilities Education Act (IDEA)) and to advocate for their right to an education.

In many facets of life, community resources are essential in helping people with autism spectrum disorder (ASD) and their families.

People with Autism Spectrum Disorder (ASD) can improve their quality of life, have access to inclusive opportunities, and reach their full potential in their communities by making use of community-based services, programs, and support networks. Building inclusive and supportive communities for people with ASD requires cooperation between community stakeholders, advocacy groups, medical professionals, educators, and families.

Difficulties in Everyday Life

1. Difficulties in Communication:
Difficulties with both verbal and nonverbal communication can affect participation in activities, social relationships, and day-to-day interactions. Limited speech, unusual speech patterns, trouble starting or carrying on conversations, and trouble comprehending metaphorical or nonliteral expressions are a few examples of possible difficulties.

2. Social Engagement and Connections:
- People with ASD frequently have trouble reading facial expressions, recognizing social cues, and having reciprocal conversations. Feelings of loneliness and isolation can result from challenges establishing and sustaining friendships, comprehending social norms, and interacting in social situations.

3. Overload and Sensory Sensitivities:
- In everyday environments, sensory sensitivities, such as increased sensitivity to light, sound, textures, smells, or tastes, can lead to discomfort, anxiety, or sensory overload. To control their reactions and handle sensory issues, people with ASD may need accommodations.

4. Schedule and Adaptability:
- Many people with ASD benefit from regular routines and may find it difficult to adjust to sudden changes or shifts. Anxiety and behavioral issues can arise from inability to

change with the times, move from one activity to another, or tolerate breaks in routine.

5. Organization and Executive Functioning:
- Problems with executive functioning, such as organizing, planning, managing time, and starting tasks, can affect daily tasks, work obligations, and academic achievement (e.g., organizing belongings, managing personal hygiene, and finishing homework).

6. Independence and Adaptive Skills:
- Daily living tasks like meal preparation, cleaning, self-care, and independent community environment navigation are all included in the category of adaptive skills. Support and education may be necessary for people with ASD to acquire the adaptive skills necessary for independent living.

7. Emotional Control and Adaptation:
- Emotional dysregulation, meltdowns, or challenging behaviors can result from difficulties controlling emotions, handling stress, and expressing feelings in an appropriate manner. Emotional well-being requires the development of powerful coping mechanisms and emotional control methods.

8. Awareness and Safety:
- People with ASD may struggle to identify safety hazards, comprehend social boundaries, and evaluate possible threats in strange environments. Promoting personal safety requires both the teaching of safety techniques and the application of methods to increase awareness and self-defense.

9. Operational Support and Service Access:
It can be difficult for people with ASD and their families to
access specialized services, therapies, educational
accommodations, and community resources because of
limited availability, cost issues, or navigating intricate care
systems.

The everyday struggles faced by people diagnosed with
autism spectrum disorder (ASD) include a variety of issues
pertaining to social interaction, communication, executive
functioning, sensory processing, and adaptive abilities.
Through identification and resolution of these obstacles via
customized interventions, accommodations, and support
networks, people with autism spectrum disorder (ASD) can
improve their capacities, manage everyday life more
skillfully, and attain increased autonomy and well-being.

Autonomy and Independence

A person with autism spectrum disorder (ASD) must be
independent and autonomous in order to develop and be
well. While the level of independence can vary based on
individual strengths, challenges, and support needs,
fostering autonomy is essential for promoting
self-confidence, life skills, and quality of life. Supporting
independence in individuals with ASD involves
recognizing strengths, providing appropriate support, and
fostering opportunities for growth across various domains.
The independence and autonomy for autism spectrum
disorder:

1. Defining Independence:
- Independence refers to the ability of an individual to
perform tasks, make decisions, and manage daily activities
with minimal assistance or support from others. It

encompasses various aspects of life skills, self-care, social interactions, and decision-making abilities.

2. Autonomy and Self-Determination:
- Autonomy involves the capacity to make choices, set goals, and advocate for one's needs and preferences. For individuals with ASD, fostering autonomy means promoting self-determination and empowering them to participate actively in decisions that affect their lives.

3. Developing Life Skills:
- Supporting independence in individuals with ASD begins with developing essential life skills across different domains, including self-care (e.g., grooming, dressing, hygiene), household tasks (e.g., cooking, cleaning), time management, money management, and community navigation.

4. Social Skills and Communication:
- Developing social skills and effective communication strategies is critical for fostering independence in social interactions, building relationships, and participating in community activities. Teaching social reciprocity, perspective-taking, and problem-solving skills enhances autonomy in social contexts.

5. Executive Functioning Skills:
- Strengthening executive functioning skills, such as planning, organization, task initiation, time management, and problem-solving, supports independence in academic, vocational, and daily life activities.

6. Adaptive Skills and Community Integration:
- Adaptive skills, including navigating public transportation, shopping independently, using technology, and accessing community resources, promote autonomy

and facilitate community integration for individuals with ASD.

7. Transition Planning and Vocational Skills:
- Transition planning focuses on preparing individuals with ASD for adulthood, including post-secondary education, employment, independent living, and community participation. Developing vocational skills, job readiness, and career exploration supports autonomy in the transition to adulthood.

8. Supportive Environments and Collaborative Approaches:
- Creating supportive environments that balance opportunities for independence with appropriate support is key to promoting autonomy in individuals with ASD. Collaborative approaches involving families, educators, therapists, and community providers enhance autonomy by addressing individual strengths and needs.

9. Self-Advocacy and Decision-Making:
- Empowering individuals with ASD to advocate for themselves, express preferences, and participate in decision-making processes fosters autonomy and self-confidence. Providing opportunities for self-advocacy training and fostering a culture of inclusion and respect supports autonomy in diverse settings.

Independence and autonomy are essential components of development and well-being for individuals with autism spectrum disorder (ASD). By focusing on strengths, developing life skills, fostering social competence, and promoting self-determination, we can empower individuals with ASD to lead fulfilling and meaningful lives, participate actively in their communities, and achieve greater autonomy and self-sufficiency.

Chapter 9: Future Directions and Research

Advances in Autism Research

Advances in autism research have significantly expanded our understanding of autism spectrum disorder (ASD), leading to improved diagnostic tools, early interventions, and targeted treatments. Ongoing research continues to unravel the complex genetic, neurobiological, and environmental factors underlying ASD, paving the way for personalized approaches to support individuals with autism and enhance their quality of life. The recent advances in autism research:

1. Genetics and Molecular Biology:
- Genetic studies have identified numerous genetic risk factors associated with autism spectrum disorder. Advances in molecular biology and genomic technologies have enabled researchers to pinpoint specific gene mutations and genetic variations linked to ASD, shedding light on the underlying biological mechanisms.

2. Neuroimaging and Brain Connectivity:
- Neuroimaging studies, such as functional magnetic resonance imaging (fMRI) and diffusion tensor imaging (DTI), have provided insights into the structural and functional connectivity patterns in the brains of individuals with ASD. These studies have identified atypical brain circuits and neural networks associated with social cognition, language processing, and sensory integration in ASD.

3. Early Detection and Diagnosis:
- Research has focused on developing more reliable and accurate tools for early detection and diagnosis of autism spectrum disorder. Advances in screening methods, such as the use of standardized behavioral assessments and biomarker studies, aim to identify signs of ASD in infancy or early childhood, enabling earlier intervention and support.

4. Behavioral Interventions and Therapies: - Research on evidence-based interventions, including applied behavior analysis (ABA), social skills training, cognitive-behavioral therapy (CBT), and developmental therapies, continues to refine therapeutic approaches for individuals with ASD. Tailored interventions based on individual strengths and needs have shown positive outcomes in improving communication, social interaction, and adaptive skills.

5. Targeted Treatments and Pharmacology:
- Advances in pharmacological research have explored potential medications to target specific symptoms and co-occurring conditions associated with autism spectrum disorder, such as anxiety, hyperactivity, and irritability. Studies on novel drug therapies and personalized medicine approaches aim to improve treatment outcomes and quality of life for individuals with ASD.

6. Environmental Risk Factors and Prevention:
- Research has investigated environmental risk factors, prenatal influences, and early developmental exposures that may contribute to the development of autism spectrum disorder. Understanding environmental influences, such as prenatal infections, maternal immune factors, and toxic exposures, informs strategies for prevention and intervention.

7. Neurodiversity and Empowerment:
- The neurodiversity paradigm emphasizes the value of diverse cognitive profiles and unique strengths among individuals with ASD. Research and advocacy efforts promoting neurodiversity advocate for inclusive education, employment opportunities, and community acceptance based on the principles of respect, empowerment, and accommodation.

8. Big Data and Collaborative Initiatives:
- Large-scale collaborative research initiatives, such as the Autism Genetic Resource Exchange (AGRE), Autism Speaks Autism Treatment Network (ATN), and Simons Foundation Autism Research Initiative (SFARI), facilitate data sharing, interdisciplinary collaboration, and translational research to accelerate progress in autism research.

Future Directions and Challenges:

Moving forward, the field of autism research aims to address persistent challenges, such as the heterogeneity of ASD, variability in treatment response, and access to services and supports. Multidisciplinary approaches integrating genetics, neuroscience, psychology, and community-based research hold promise for advancing our understanding of autism spectrum disorder and improving outcomes for individuals and families affected by ASD.

Recent advances in autism research have revolutionized our understanding of autism spectrum disorder (ASD) and informed innovative approaches to diagnosis, intervention, and support. By leveraging emerging technologies, collaborative partnerships, and personalized strategies, researchers are striving to enhance the lives of individuals with ASD and promote greater inclusion, acceptance, and empowerment within society.

Promising Treatments and Therapies

Promising treatments and therapies for autism spectrum disorder (ASD) encompass a diverse range of approaches aimed at addressing core symptoms, improving functional abilities, and enhancing overall quality of life for individuals with ASD. While there is no one-size-fits-all treatment for ASD due to its heterogeneity, ongoing research and clinical innovations have identified effective interventions that can benefit individuals across the spectrum. some promising treatments and therapies for autism spectrum disorder:

1. ABA, or applied behavior analysis:
- ABA is a well-established, evidence-based therapy that focuses on

modifying behaviors by breaking down tasks into manageable steps and providing positive reinforcement for desired behaviors. ABA targets specific skills such as communication, social interaction, adaptive behaviors, and reduction of challenging behaviors.

2. Early Intensive Behavioral Intervention (EIBI):
- EIBI involves intensive ABA therapy delivered at an early age, typically before age 5, to promote rapid skill acquisition and developmental progress. EIBI aims to capitalize on the brain's neuroplasticity during critical periods of development and enhance long-term outcomes.

3. Teaching Social Skills:
- Social skills training programs target deficits in social communication, reciprocal interaction, and understanding social cues. These interventions use structured activities,

role-playing, peer modeling, and video modeling to teach social skills and promote social competence.

4. Language and Speech Therapy:
- Speech-language therapy focuses on improving communication skills, including speech production, language comprehension, pragmatic language (use of language in social contexts), and alternative communication methods (e.g., augmentative and alternative communication – AAC systems).

5. OT (Occupational Therapy):
- Occupational therapists work with individuals with ASD to enhance sensory processing, motor coordination, self-care skills, and participation in daily activities. OT interventions may include sensory integration therapy, fine motor activities, and adaptive strategies for independent living.

6. CBT: Cognitive-behavioral therapy
- CBT is a therapeutic approach that helps individuals with ASD manage anxiety, reduce repetitive behaviors, and develop coping strategies for emotional regulation. CBT techniques include cognitive restructuring, relaxation training, and exposure therapy.

7. Medications for Development:
- Developmental therapies focus on fostering overall development and adaptive skills through play-based interventions, structured activities, and family-centered approaches. These therapies promote cognitive, language, social, and motor skills in a supportive environment.

8. Technology-Assisted Interventions:
- Innovative technologies, such as virtual reality (VR), computer-based training programs, and mobile apps, are being utilized to deliver personalized interventions and support cognitive, communication, and social skills development in individuals with ASD.

9. Parent-Mediated and Family-Centered Approaches:
- Parent training programs empower parents and caregivers to implement effective strategies, promote positive behaviors, and support their child's development at home and in the community. Family-centered approaches emphasize collaboration, shared decision-making, and holistic support for the entire family unit.

10. Medication and Pharmacological Treatments:
- Pharmacological interventions may be prescribed to manage specific symptoms or co-occurring conditions associated with autism spectrum disorder, such as anxiety, ADHD, or sleep disturbances. Medications should be carefully monitored and prescribed by healthcare professionals.

Promising treatments and therapies for autism spectrum disorder (ASD) focus on addressing core symptoms, enhancing functional abilities, and supporting overall well-being in individuals across the lifespan. Tailored interventions based on individual strengths, needs, and preferences, along with early identification and multidisciplinary collaboration, contribute to positive outcomes and improved quality of life for individuals with ASD and their families.

Chapter 10: Advocacy And Awareness

Advocacy Initiatives

Advocacy initiatives for autism spectrum disorder (ASD) encompass efforts to promote awareness, acceptance, inclusion, and support for individuals with ASD and their families. Advocates work to advance policies, programs, and resources that enhance access to education, healthcare, employment, and community services for individuals across the autism spectrum. By raising awareness, advocating for rights, and fostering collaboration, advocacy initiatives aim to empower individuals with ASD and promote a more inclusive society. The consist of:

1. Raising Awareness and Education:
- Advocacy organizations and campaigns raise public awareness about autism spectrum disorder, dispel myths and misconceptions, and promote understanding of diverse abilities and strengths among individuals with ASD. Educational initiatives focus on disseminating accurate information, promoting early intervention, and fostering inclusive practices in schools and communities.

2. Promoting Access to Services and Supports:
- Advocates work to improve access to comprehensive services, therapies, and support for individuals with ASD and their families. This includes advocating for affordable healthcare, specialized education programs, behavioral interventions, vocational training, and community-based resources tailored to the needs of individuals across the spectrum.

3.Legislative and Policy Advocacy:

- Advocacy efforts seek to influence public policy, legislation, and funding priorities to address the needs of individuals with ASD and ensure their rights are protected. This includes advocating for disability rights, insurance coverage for autism-related services, employment opportunities, and housing accommodations.

4. Employment and Vocational Advocacy:
- Advocates promote inclusive employment practices and advocate for vocational training, job coaching, and supported employment programs for individuals with ASD. They work with employers to create autism-friendly workplaces that accommodate diverse strengths and abilities.

5. Supporting Transition to Adulthood:
- Advocacy initiatives focus on supporting the transition of individuals with ASD to adulthood by advocating for post-secondary education opportunities, independent living skills training, community integration programs, and access to supportive housing and transportation services.

6. Family Support and Empowerment:
- Advocates empower families of individuals with ASD by providing information, resources, and support networks. Family advocacy initiatives emphasize parent education, advocacy training, and peer support to navigate systems of care, access services, and advocate for their child's rights and needs.

7. Autistic Self-Advocacy and Representation:
- Autistic self-advocates play a critical role in advocating for their rights, preferences, and inclusion in decision-making processes. Self-advocacy initiatives

empower individuals with ASD to share their lived experiences, challenge stigma, and advocate for policies that prioritize their autonomy and well-being.

8. Community Engagement and Collaboration:
- Advocacy initiatives foster collaboration among stakeholders, including individuals with ASD, families, educators, healthcare providers, policymakers, and community leaders. Collaborative efforts promote community engagement, shared resources, and innovative solutions to address the diverse needs of individuals with ASD.

Advocacy initiatives for autism spectrum disorder (ASD) are essential for promoting awareness, acceptance, inclusion, and support within society. By advocating for rights, access to services, and opportunities for individuals with ASD, advocates contribute to creating a more equitable and inclusive world where individuals across the spectrum can thrive, participate fully, and achieve their potential.

Strategies for Reducing Stigma Associated with Autism Spectrum Disorder (ASD)

Reducing stigma associated with autism spectrum disorder (ASD) is crucial for fostering understanding, acceptance, and inclusion of individuals with ASD within society. Stigma arises from misconceptions, stereotypes, and negative attitudes toward autism, leading to discrimination, social exclusion, and barriers to opportunities for individuals across the spectrum. Efforts to reduce stigma focus on promoting awareness, education, empathy, and positive representation of autism to create a more supportive and inclusive environment. Approaches for reducing stigma related to autism spectrum disorder:

1. Education and Awareness Campaigns:
- Education initiatives aim to dispel myths, increase understanding, and promote accurate information about autism spectrum disorder. Awareness campaigns raise public awareness about the diversity of abilities and strengths among individuals with ASD, emphasizing the importance of acceptance and inclusion.

2. Promoting Positive Representation:
- Promoting positive portrayals of individuals with ASD in media, literature, and popular culture helps challenge stereotypes and promote empathy and understanding. Highlighting the unique talents, perspectives, and contributions of individuals with ASD fosters acceptance and reduces stigma.

3. Autistic Self-Advocacy and Empowerment:
- Amplifying the voices and perspectives of autistic self-advocates empowers individuals with ASD to share their experiences, challenge stigma, and advocate for their rights and needs. Autistic-led initiatives promote self-determination, autonomy, and respect for diverse cognitive profiles.

4. Inclusive Education and Employment Practices:
- Promoting inclusive education and employment practices that accommodate diverse learning styles, communication preferences, and support needs helps create environments where individuals with ASD can thrive and contribute. Providing reasonable accommodations and promoting neurodiversity in educational and workplace settings reduces stigma and fosters inclusion.

5. Community Engagement and Collaboration:
- Engaging communities, stakeholders, and organizations in collaborative efforts to address stigma and promote acceptance of individuals with ASD is essential. Building partnerships, sharing resources, and fostering dialogue create opportunities for collective action and positive change.

6. Professional Training and Development:
- Providing training and professional development opportunities for educators, healthcare providers, and service providers on autism awareness and best practices in supporting individuals with ASD promotes more inclusive and informed approaches. Equipping professionals with knowledge and skills reduces stigma and enhances support for individuals with ASD.

7. Supporting Families and Caregivers:
- Providing support, resources, and empowerment for families and caregivers of individuals with ASD helps address stigma and promotes resilience. Family advocacy initiatives emphasize education, peer support, and community engagement to navigate challenges and advocate for inclusive policies and services.

8. Cultural Competence and Diversity Awareness:
- Promoting cultural competence and awareness of diversity within the autism community helps address intersectional stigma and promote inclusive practices across different cultural, linguistic, and ethnic backgrounds.
Reducing stigma associated with autism spectrum disorder (ASD) requires concerted efforts to promote education, awareness, empathy, and inclusion within society. By challenging stereotypes, amplifying diverse voices,

fostering collaboration, and promoting positive representation, we can create a more accepting and supportive environment where individuals with ASD are valued for their unique abilities and contributions.

Strategies for Encouraging Individuals with Autism Spectrum Disorder (ASD)

Encouraging individuals with autism spectrum disorder (ASD) involves fostering their strengths, promoting self-confidence, and providing support to help them navigate challenges and achieve their goals. Encouragement plays a crucial role in empowering individuals with ASD to build resilience, develop skills, and participate actively in their communities. By creating a nurturing and supportive environment, we can inspire individuals with ASD to embrace their potential and pursue meaningful opportunities. Use these strategies for encouraging and supporting individuals with autism spectrum disorder:

1. Identify and Celebrate Strengths:

   - Recognize and celebrate the unique strengths, talents, and interests of individuals with ASD. Encouragement begins by acknowledging their abilities and providing opportunities for them to showcase their talents in areas such as art, music, technology, or academics.

2. Set Realistic Goals and Expectations:

   - Work collaboratively with individuals with ASD to set achievable goals based on their interests and abilities. Break tasks into manageable steps, provide clear instructions, and offer positive reinforcement and praise for progress and effort.

3. Provide Structure and Routine:

- Establish consistent routines and structured environments that promote predictability and reduce anxiety for individuals with ASD. Clear schedules, visual supports, and explicit expectations help create a sense of security and enable individuals to thrive.

4. Use Positive Reinforcement and Feedback:

- Encourage positive behaviors and efforts through praise, rewards, and positive reinforcement. Provide specific, constructive feedback to help individuals understand their strengths and areas for growth.

5. Promote Self-Advocacy and Decision-Making:

- Empower individuals with ASD to express their preferences, make choices, and advocate for their needs and preferences. Encourage self-determination and decision-making to foster independence and confidence.

6. Offer Opportunities for Social Interaction:

- Create inclusive social opportunities that allow individuals with ASD to practice social skills, build friendships, and develop meaningful connections. Structured activities, peer support groups, and cooperative games can promote social engagement and communication.

7. Provide Accommodations and Support:

- Offer appropriate accommodations and support tailored to the individual's needs and preferences. This may include assistive technologies, sensory supports, visual aids, or modified learning environments to optimize success and participation.

8. Encourage Healthy Coping Strategies:

   - Teach and model effective coping strategies for managing stress, anxiety, and sensory sensitivities. Encourage activities that promote relaxation, self-regulation, and emotional well-being, such as mindfulness, sensory breaks, or physical exercise.

9. Promote Inclusive Education and Employment Opportunities:

   - Advocate for inclusive education and employment practices that value diversity and accommodate individuals with ASD. Foster partnerships with schools, employers, and community organizations to create supportive environments and pathways for success.

10. Celebrate Milestones and Progress:

   - Acknowledge and celebrate achievements, milestones, and personal growth. Recognize efforts and resilience, and encourage a growth mindset that values continuous improvement and learning

Encouraging individuals with autism spectrum disorder (ASD) involves fostering strengths, promoting self-confidence, and providing support tailored to their needs and preferences. By embracing a strengths-based approach, promoting self-determination, and creating inclusive environments, we can empower individuals with ASD to thrive, build meaningful connections, and pursue their aspirations.

Individuals with autism spectrum disorder (ASD) and their families.

I wish you all well on your journey of understanding, acceptance, and empowerment. Living with ASD presents unique challenges, but it also encompasses incredible strengths, talents, and perspectives that enrich our world. May you find the support, resources, and encouragement you need to navigate life with resilience, confidence, and joy.

Remember that each individual with ASD is unique, with their own set of abilities and potential. Together, let's continue to promote awareness, advocate for inclusion, and celebrate the diverse strengths and contributions of individuals across the autism spectrum. May you find kindness, understanding, and acceptance in your communities. Keep striving for progress, celebrating achievements, and embracing each step forward. You are valued, you are capable, and you are deserving of every opportunity to thrive. Please don't forget to leave a review to encourage me in bringing forth more up-to-date information, I will appreciate it.

Wishing you all the best on your journey